EMMANUEL JOSEPH

Digital Dominance and Land Legacies, Comparing the Strategies of Tech Leaders and Real Estate Magnates

Copyright © 2025 by Emmanuel Joseph

All rights reserved. No part of this publication may be reproduced, stored or transmitted in any form or by any means, electronic, mechanical, photocopying, recording, scanning, or otherwise without written permission from the publisher. It is illegal to copy this book, post it to a website, or distribute it by any other means without permission.

First edition

This book was professionally typeset on Reedsy. Find out more at reedsy.com

Contents

1	Chapter 1	1
2	Chapter 1: The Dawn of Digital Giants	3
3	Chapter 2: The Age of Real Estate Magnates	5
4	Chapter 3: Visionary Leadership	7
5	Chapter 4: Innovation and Adaptation	9
6	Chapter 5: Risk and Reward	11
7	Chapter 6: Financial Strategies	13
8	Chapter 7: Market Influence	15
9	Chapter 8: Technological Advancements	17
10	Chapter 9: Strategic Partnerships	19
11	Chapter 10: Regulatory Challenges	21
12	Chapter 11: Social Responsibility	23
13	Chapter 12: Legacy and Impact	25

1

Chapter 1

Introduction

In the dynamic landscape of the 21st century, two formidable forces have emerged as pivotal shapers of the modern world: tech leaders and real estate magnates. These visionaries, though operating in vastly different realms, share a common thread of ambition, innovation, and strategic prowess. The digital revolution, spearheaded by tech titans, has redefined industries, disrupted traditional business models, and transformed the way we live and interact. Meanwhile, real estate magnates have continued to shape the physical world, developing iconic structures and urban environments that stand as testaments to human ingenuity and resilience.

The rise of digital giants like Google, Amazon, and Facebook marks a new era of technological dominance. These companies, driven by relentless innovation and a keen understanding of market dynamics, have created ecosystems that touch every aspect of our lives. From e-commerce and social media to cloud computing and artificial intelligence, tech leaders have revolutionized the way we work, communicate, and entertain ourselves. Their ability to foresee trends and adapt to a rapidly changing environment has positioned them at the forefront of global economic power.

On the other hand, the world of real estate remains a cornerstone of economic stability and growth. Real estate magnates, with their keen eye for valuable assets and strategic investments, have played a crucial role in urban development and economic expansion. Their ventures have not only generated immense wealth but also provided essential infrastructure, housing, and commercial spaces that support thriving communities. The physicality of real estate offers a stark contrast to the intangible nature of digital assets, yet both sectors demand a profound understanding of market forces and consumer behavior.

As we delve into the comparative strategies of these influential leaders, it becomes evident that their paths, while distinct, are also remarkably intertwined. The intersection of technology and real estate offers unique opportunities for innovation and collaboration. Smart cities, sustainable developments, and tech-integrated infrastructure exemplify the synergies between these two domains. By examining the approaches of tech leaders and real estate magnates, we gain valuable insights into the future of business, urbanization, and societal advancement.

This exploration is not merely an academic exercise but a quest to understand the driving forces behind contemporary success. By analyzing the visionary leadership, financial acumen, and adaptive strategies of these remarkable individuals, we uncover the blueprint for navigating an increasingly complex and interconnected world. "Digital Dominance and Land Legacies" invites readers to embark on a journey through the realms of technology and real estate, unraveling the secrets of those who shape our present and define our future.

2

Chapter 1: The Dawn of Digital Giants

The dawn of the 21st century marked the rise of a new breed of leaders—tech titans whose innovations reshaped the world. Companies like Google, Amazon, and Facebook were founded by visionary minds who saw the potential of digital technologies. These leaders didn't just create products; they revolutionized the way we live, work, and interact.

The digital revolution was characterized by a rapid pace of innovation, driven by a relentless pursuit of efficiency and connectivity. Tech leaders were not just entrepreneurs; they were pioneers charting unknown territories. Their vision and determination propelled the world into the digital age.

As the internet became more accessible, these tech giants leveraged their platforms to create ecosystems that connected billions of people. Social media, e-commerce, and cloud computing became the cornerstones of modern society. The impact of their innovations was profound, transforming industries and daily life.

Yet, the journey was not without challenges. Competition was fierce, and the race to stay ahead required constant adaptation and innovation. The tech leaders navigated regulatory hurdles, security concerns, and ethical dilemmas, shaping the digital landscape with their decisions.

Today, the legacy of these digital pioneers continues to evolve. Their companies remain at the forefront of technological advancements, influencing the way we live, work, and communicate. The story of the dawn of digital giants is a testament to the power of vision and innovation.

Chapter 2: The Age of Real Estate Magnates

Long before the digital era, real estate magnates laid the foundation for modern cities and economies. Figures like Donald Trump, Conrad Hilton, and Leona Helmsley leveraged land and property to build empires. Real estate, unlike the digital realm, was a tangible asset that required a different set of strategies.

These magnates understood the importance of location, market trends, and economic cycles. Their success was built on vision, risk-taking, and a keen understanding of urban development and human needs. They transformed landscapes and created landmarks that defined cities.

The real estate industry thrived on its ability to adapt to changing economic conditions. Magnates like John D. Rockefeller and Samuel Zell capitalized on market opportunities, turning properties into profitable ventures. They demonstrated the art of negotiation and deal-making, often turning around failing properties into success stories.

However, the path to success was not without obstacles. Economic downturns, regulatory changes, and competition posed significant challenges. Real estate magnates navigated these hurdles with resilience and strategic planning, leaving a lasting impact on the industry.

Their legacies are etched in the skylines of major cities. The buildings and developments they created stand as testaments to their vision and determination. The age of real estate magnates showcases the power of tangible assets and strategic foresight.

4

Chapter 3: Visionary Leadership

Both tech leaders and real estate magnates share a common trait: visionary leadership. Visionaries like Jeff Bezos and Elon Musk redefined industries through their innovative approaches and bold ambitions. Similarly, real estate magnates like Stephen Ross and Sam Zell transformed urban landscapes with their foresight and daring investments.

Visionary leadership involves seeing opportunities where others see obstacles. These leaders predicted future trends and shaped them. Their ability to think ahead and take calculated risks set them apart from their peers. They were not afraid to challenge the status quo and pursue their dreams relentlessly.

In the tech industry, visionary leaders drove innovation through cutting-edge technologies and disruptive business models. They leveraged their platforms to create new markets and redefine existing ones. Their impact extended beyond their companies, influencing entire industries and shaping the future.

Real estate magnates, on the other hand, showcased their vision through large-scale developments and urban transformations. They understood the potential of underdeveloped areas and turned them into thriving communities. Their projects not only generated wealth but also created lasting legacies for future generations.

The stories of visionary leaders in both sectors highlight the importance of foresight, innovation, and bold decision-making. Their contributions have left an indelible mark on the world, inspiring future generations to dream big and think differently.

5

Chapter 4: Innovation and Adaptation

Innovation is at the heart of the digital realm. Tech leaders continuously push the boundaries of what's possible, driving advancements in AI, cloud computing, and more. In contrast, real estate magnates innovate through architecture, design, and sustainability.

Both sectors require constant adaptation to changing market conditions and consumer needs. The ability to innovate and adapt is crucial for long-term success. Tech leaders introduced revolutionary products and services, transforming the way we interact with technology. They embraced emerging trends and incorporated them into their business strategies.

Real estate magnates, on the other hand, focused on creating sustainable and efficient properties. They adopted green building practices, smart technologies, and innovative designs to enhance the value of their developments. Their ability to adapt to changing market demands and economic cycles ensured their continued success.

The intersection of innovation and adaptation is evident in the strategies of both tech leaders and real estate magnates. They recognized the importance of staying ahead of the curve and continuously evolving their approaches. Their ability to foresee future trends and pivot accordingly allowed them to maintain their competitive edge.

Innovation and adaptation are key drivers of progress in both sectors. The relentless pursuit of new ideas and the willingness to embrace change have propelled tech leaders and real estate magnates to new heights. Their stories underscore the importance of creativity, resilience, and strategic thinking in achieving long-term success.

6

Chapter 5: Risk and Reward

The paths to success for both tech leaders and real estate magnates are fraught with risks. In the tech world, startups face high failure rates, and established companies must constantly evolve to stay relevant. The real estate market, on the other hand, is subject to economic fluctuations and regulatory challenges.

However, with great risk comes great reward. Successful tech leaders and real estate magnates have amassed vast fortunes, but their journeys are also marked by failures and setbacks. Understanding and managing risk is a key component of their strategies. They approached risk with calculated decision-making and strategic planning.

In the tech industry, entrepreneurs took bold risks to disrupt established markets and create new ones. They navigated uncharted territories and faced intense competition. Their ability to take risks and learn from failures paved the way for their eventual success.

Real estate magnates, on the other hand, managed risks associated with property investments, market cycles, and regulatory changes. They demonstrated resilience in the face of economic downturns and leveraged their expertise to turn challenges into opportunities. Their ability to manage risk and capitalize on market conditions contributed to their enduring success.

The stories of risk and reward in both sectors highlight the importance of resilience, strategic planning, and a willingness to take bold steps. Successful leaders in both tech and real estate recognized that risk is an inherent part of growth and embraced it as a necessary element of their journey.

7

Chapter 6: Financial Strategies

Tech leaders often rely on venture capital, IPOs, and strategic partnerships to fuel growth. Their financial strategies are geared towards rapid expansion and market dominance. Companies like Google and Facebook initially relied on venture capital to get off the ground, eventually going public to access greater capital and fund their ambitious projects.

On the other hand, real estate magnates focus on leveraging debt, equity, and investment portfolios. Their financial strategies aim for long-term stability and asset appreciation. Real estate moguls like Sam Zell and Stephen Ross have mastered the art of using leverage to maximize returns on property investments, balancing risk and reward effectively.

Both groups of leaders demonstrate a deep understanding of financial management, though their approaches differ significantly. Tech companies often reinvest profits into research and development to stay ahead in a rapidly changing industry. In contrast, real estate magnates prioritize asset management and long-term planning to ensure steady cash flow and growth.

Despite their differences, both tech leaders and real estate magnates recognize the importance of financial innovation. By exploring new funding mechanisms and investment opportunities, they have built resilient business models capable of withstanding economic fluctuations.

The financial strategies employed by tech leaders and real estate magnates highlight their adaptability and foresight. They continually evolve their approaches to remain competitive, ensuring their continued success in dynamic markets.

8

Chapter 7: Market Influence

Tech leaders wield significant influence over global markets. Companies like Apple and Microsoft not only dominate their industries but also shape consumer behavior and economic trends. Their products and services have become integral parts of daily life, driving demand and influencing global supply chains.

Real estate magnates, on the other hand, influence local and national economies through their developments and investments. Their projects create jobs, stimulate economic growth, and shape urban landscapes. The construction of iconic buildings and large-scale developments can transform entire neighborhoods and cities.

Both tech and real estate leaders have the power to drive economic growth, create jobs, and influence policies. Their market influence extends beyond their respective industries, impacting the broader economy. Tech companies, for example, can affect stock markets and investor sentiment, while real estate developments can boost local economies and property values.

The influence of tech leaders and real estate magnates underscores their pivotal roles in shaping modern society. Their decisions and actions have far-reaching consequences, affecting not only their industries but also the lives of millions of people around the world.

Understanding the market influence of these leaders provides valuable insights into the interconnected nature of the global economy. Their ability to drive change and innovation highlights the importance of strategic leadership in achieving long-term success.

9

Chapter 8: Technological Advancements

Tech leaders are at the forefront of technological advancements. They drive innovations that revolutionize industries, from AI and robotics to renewable energy and space exploration. Companies like Tesla and SpaceX, led by Elon Musk, are pushing the boundaries of what is possible, transforming transportation and energy sectors.

Real estate magnates also embrace technology, incorporating smart systems, green building practices, and advanced construction techniques. Innovations in real estate technology, such as PropTech, are enhancing efficiency, sustainability, and tenant experience. Smart buildings, for example, use IoT devices to optimize energy consumption and improve security.

The integration of technology in real estate enhances efficiency, sustainability, and tenant experience. Both sectors benefit from technological advancements, though the applications and impacts differ. While tech companies focus on creating cutting-edge products and services, real estate leaders use technology to improve the value and functionality of their properties.

Technological advancements are driving the future of both industries, enabling leaders to stay competitive and meet evolving market demands. The adoption of innovative technologies is essential for maintaining growth and achieving long-term success in a rapidly changing world.

The stories of tech leaders and real estate magnates highlight the transformative power of technology. Their commitment to innovation and progress is reshaping industries and creating new opportunities for growth and development.

10

Chapter 9: Strategic Partnerships

Strategic partnerships are crucial for both tech leaders and real estate magnates. In the tech world, collaborations with other companies, universities, and research institutions drive innovation and growth. Partnerships between tech giants like Apple and IBM have led to groundbreaking advancements and expanded market reach.

Real estate magnates form partnerships with developers, investors, and local governments to execute large-scale projects. These collaborations leverage complementary strengths and resources, enabling leaders to achieve their goals more effectively. Joint ventures, for example, allow real estate developers to pool resources and share risks, making it easier to undertake ambitious projects.

Collaboration is a common thread that links the strategies of tech and real estate leaders. By working together, they can overcome challenges, accelerate innovation, and create value. Strategic partnerships also foster a culture of learning and growth, enabling leaders to stay ahead in competitive markets.

The importance of strategic partnerships cannot be overstated. They provide access to new resources, markets, and expertise, helping leaders to achieve their visions and drive progress. Successful partnerships are built on trust, mutual benefit, and a shared commitment to excellence.

Both tech leaders and real estate magnates recognize the value of collaboration in achieving long-term success. Their ability to forge strategic partnerships has been instrumental in their growth and impact on their respective industries and beyond.

11

Chapter 10: Regulatory Challenges

Both tech leaders and real estate magnates face regulatory challenges that impact their operations. The tech industry grapples with issues like data privacy, antitrust laws, and intellectual property rights. Companies like Facebook and Google have faced scrutiny and legal battles over their practices, highlighting the complex regulatory landscape of the digital world.

Real estate magnates navigate zoning laws, environmental regulations, and property taxes. The approval process for large-scale developments often involves negotiating with local authorities and addressing community concerns. Compliance with environmental regulations, for example, is crucial for sustainable development and can affect project timelines and costs.

Understanding and influencing regulatory environments is a key aspect of their strategies. Successful leaders in both sectors are adept at navigating these challenges and leveraging them to their advantage. They invest in legal expertise and advocacy efforts to stay compliant and shape favorable regulatory conditions.

Regulatory challenges present both risks and opportunities. Leaders who can anticipate and adapt to regulatory changes are better positioned to succeed. Their ability to influence policy and engage with stakeholders is a testament to their strategic acumen and resilience.

The stories of tech leaders and real estate magnates highlight the importance of regulatory awareness and adaptability. Their success depends on their ability to navigate complex legal landscapes and align their strategies with evolving regulatory frameworks.

This book explores the strategies and impacts of tech leaders and real estate magnates, highlighting the similarities and differences in their approaches to achieving success. Through visionary leadership, innovation, and strategic partnerships, these leaders have left an indelible mark on their respective industries and the world at large.

12

Chapter 11: Social Responsibility

Tech leaders and real estate magnates increasingly recognize the importance of social responsibility. Companies like Microsoft and Google invest in initiatives that address global challenges such as climate change and digital inclusion. Their efforts include reducing carbon footprints, promoting renewable energy, and supporting education and workforce development in underserved communities.

Real estate magnates focus on sustainable development, affordable housing, and community engagement. They adopt green building practices to minimize environmental impact and create energy-efficient structures. Additionally, they contribute to local communities by developing public spaces, supporting local businesses, and providing affordable housing options.

Both groups of leaders understand that their actions have far-reaching social impacts. By prioritizing social responsibility, they enhance their reputations, build trust with stakeholders, and contribute to the greater good. These efforts are not only ethically sound but also beneficial for long-term business success.

Social responsibility initiatives also provide opportunities for collaboration and innovation. Tech companies partner with nonprofits, governments, and other organizations to address complex social issues. Real estate developers collaborate with community groups and local authorities to ensure their projects meet the needs of residents and promote inclusivity.

The commitment to social responsibility reflects the evolving role of business leaders in society. Tech leaders and real estate magnates recognize that their influence extends beyond profit margins, and they strive to make positive contributions to the world. Their efforts demonstrate the potential for businesses to drive meaningful change and create a better future for all.

13

Chapter 12: Legacy and Impact

The legacies of tech leaders and real estate magnates are defined by their contributions to their industries and society. Tech leaders leave behind a legacy of innovation, shaping the future through their technological advancements. Companies like Apple, Amazon, and Tesla have revolutionized industries, setting new standards for what is possible and inspiring future generations of entrepreneurs.

Real estate magnates leave a physical legacy, transforming skylines and urban landscapes. The iconic buildings and developments they create become landmarks and symbols of progress. Their contributions to urban planning and development have lasting impacts on cities and communities, influencing how people live, work, and interact.

Both groups of leaders have a lasting impact on the world, influencing how we live, work, and interact. Their stories are a testament to the power of vision, innovation, and leadership. Through their achievements, they have demonstrated the importance of ambition, resilience, and strategic thinking in achieving success.

The legacies of these leaders also highlight the interconnectedness of different industries. Technological advancements drive demand for new types of real estate, while urban development creates opportunities for tech companies to expand and innovate. The synergy between tech leaders and real estate magnates contributes to the dynamic growth and evolution of modern society.

Ultimately, the legacy of tech leaders and real estate magnates is not just measured by their financial success but by the enduring impact of their work. Their ability to envision and realize transformative ideas has shaped the world in profound ways, leaving a lasting imprint on future generations. Their stories serve as inspiration for aspiring leaders, reminding us of the importance of vision, innovation, and the pursuit of excellence.

Book Description: Digital Dominance and Land Legacies: Comparing the Strategies of Tech Leaders and Real Estate Magnates

"Digital Dominance and Land Legacies" delves into the fascinating world of tech leaders and real estate magnates, exploring their unique strategies for achieving success. The book provides an in-depth comparison of the visionary approaches, innovative tactics, and strategic partnerships that define these two influential groups.

Through twelve captivating chapters, readers will discover how tech titans like Jeff Bezos and Elon Musk have revolutionized industries with their groundbreaking innovations. From the rise of digital giants to the relentless pursuit of technological advancements, the book highlights the impact of their visionary leadership.

Simultaneously, the book traces the journeys of real estate moguls such as Donald Trump and Conrad Hilton, who have transformed urban landscapes with their strategic investments and developments. It examines their ability to navigate economic cycles, regulatory challenges, and market trends to build lasting legacies.

Each chapter uncovers the parallels and contrasts between the digital and real estate realms, shedding light on the importance of risk-taking, financial acumen, and social responsibility. The narrative emphasizes how both tech leaders and real estate magnates leverage strategic partnerships and innovation to drive progress and create enduring value.

"Digital Dominance and Land Legacies" is a compelling exploration of two distinct yet interconnected worlds, offering readers valuable insights into the minds of some of the most influential leaders of our time. Whether you're an aspiring entrepreneur, a seasoned professional, or simply curious about the

CHAPTER 12: LEGACY AND IMPACT

forces shaping our modern society, this book provides a thought-provoking journey through the strategies and legacies of tech and real estate visionaries.

www.ingramcontent.com/pod-product-compliance
Lightning Source LLC
LaVergne TN
LVHW020741090526
838202LV00057BA/6171